WHEREVER YOU ♥ GO

ALEXIS DAVIS

ILLUSTRATED BY

EMILY HAMMOND

ISBN 978-1-63814-549-3 (Paperback)
ISBN 978-1-63814-550-9 (Hardcover)
ISBN 978-1-63814-551-6 (Digital)

Covenant Books, Inc.
11661 Hwy 707
Murrells Inlet, SC 29576
www.covenantbooks.com

For Bodie Zayne—my inspiration. You're my favorite thing in the world!

For forty years God's people had been without homes;
All around the desert they meandered and roamed.
Then God said to Joshua, "Rise up! Take a stand!
It's time for My people to inherit their land!"[1]

---

[1] Joshua 1:2 (NLT), "Moses my servant is dead. Therefore, the time has come for you to lead these people, the Israelites, across the Jordan River into the land I am giving them. I promise you what I promised Moses: 'Wherever you set foot, you will be on land I have given you.'"

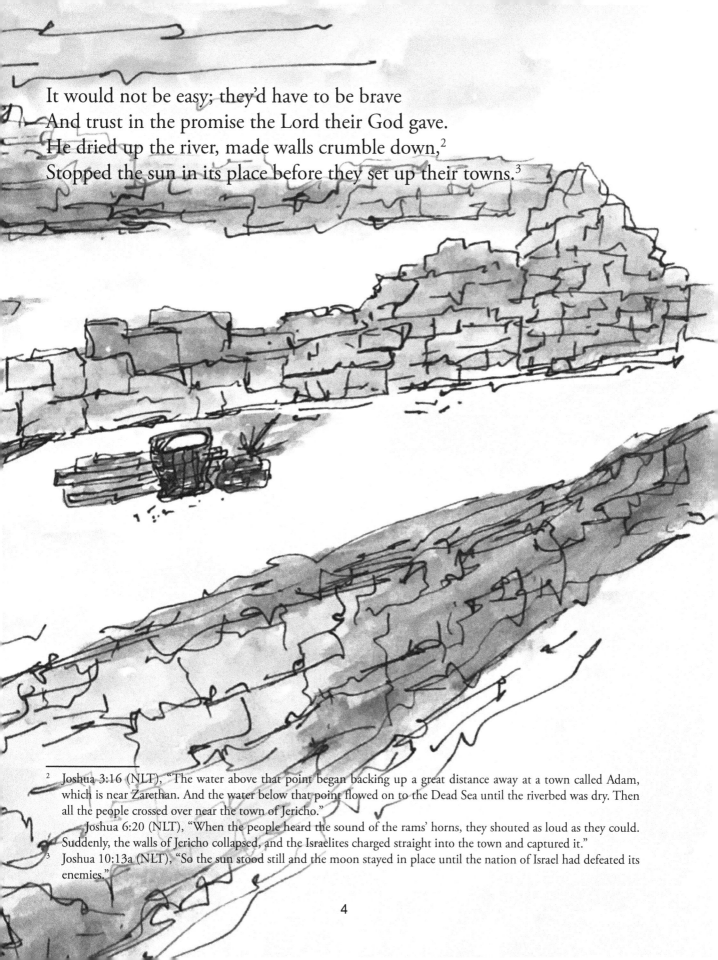

It would not be easy; they'd have to be brave
And trust in the promise the Lord their God gave.
He dried up the river, made walls crumble down,[2]
Stopped the sun in its place before they set up their towns.[3]

---

[2] Joshua 3:16 (NLT), "The water above that point began backing up a great distance away at a town called Adam, which is near Zarethan. And the water below that point flowed on to the Dead Sea until the riverbed was dry. Then all the people crossed over near the town of Jericho."

Joshua 6:20 (NLT), "When the people heard the sound of the rams' horns, they shouted as loud as they could. Suddenly, the walls of Jericho collapsed, and the Israelites charged straight into the town and captured it."

[3] Joshua 10:13a (NLT), "So the sun stood still and the moon stayed in place until the nation of Israel had defeated its enemies."

God gave them their enemies into their hands,[4]
And his people acquired their great Promised Land!
He told them repeatedly to not be afraid,
And although it wasn't easy, the people obeyed.

[4] Joshua 12:7–24 (NLT), "In all, thirty-one kings were defeated."

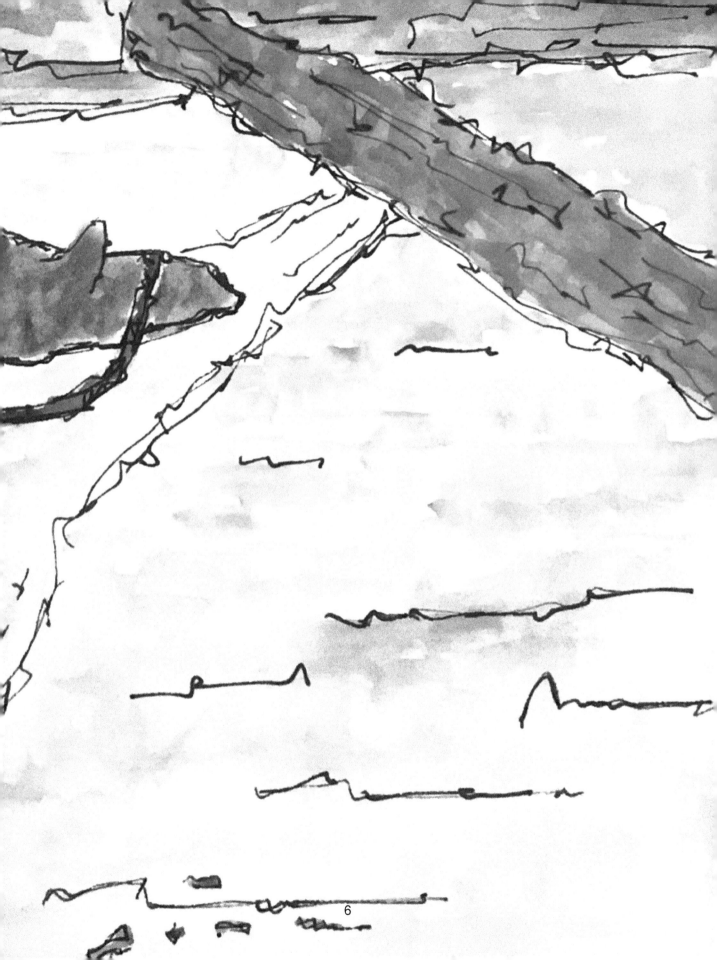

He said He'd be with them and He would provide,
There was no need to worry, to fear, or to hide.
Sometimes it is scary to do something new,
But this message for Joshua is meant for you too!

You may one day get to take a trip on a plane
To visit your family that lives far away.
Your luggage is packed and your ticket's in hand;
You look out the window as giant planes land.

"Those wings are so long and those wheels are so tiny!
What if on takeoff I get scared and start crying?
Will it be dark, cold, or bumpy up there?
How does that huge plane even stay in the air?"

It takes off a bit shaky; then you're up in the clouds!
The pilot announces, "All is now safe and sound!"
And the view from your window doesn't even cause fright,
For God's world from above is a beautiful sight![5]

---

[5]   Isaiah 42:5–6a (ESV), "Thus says God, the Lord, who created the heavens and stretched them out, who spread out the earth and what comes from it; who gives breath to the people on it and spirit to those who walk in it: "I am the Lord; I have called you in righteousness; I will take you by the hand and keep you."

Your lunch is all packed and your new shoes look cool!
It's very exciting, the first day of school!
But here comes the bus with its yellow lights flashing,
And quick as can be, the fears start attacking:

COOKIES

BACK TO
SCHOOL!

Materials:

"How will I know when it's time to get off?
What if I get on the wrong bus and get lost?
I might have to sit all alone, and still more,
What if my feet don't quite reach the floor?"

But the bus driver smiles. "Here's a seat just for you!"
And at the very next stop, your best friend climbs on too!⁶

---

⁶ Ecclesiastes 4:9–10 (ESV), "Two are better than one, because they have a good reward for their toil. For if they fall, one will lift up his fellow. But woe to him who is alone when he falls and has not another to lift him up!"

Your team won the game! Now you get the distinction
Of marching in a parade as your recognition.
You'll wear matching shirts and toss candy to children
And people will be there to cheer by the millions!

Although it's exciting, this honor you've been bestowed,
On the way there the worries may just start to grow:
"What if the marching band's drums are too loud?
And if I can't find my mom's face in the crowd?"[7]

7   Isaiah 41:10 (NLT), "Don't be afraid, for I am with you. Don't be discouraged, for I am your God. I will strengthen you and help you. I will hold you up with my victorious right hand."

There's no need to let these fears cause you concern.
Remember brave Joshua and the lesson he learned?
God told him not to fear, he would not be alone;
Remember this promise! Claim it as your own![8]

So if you fly on a plane or march in a parade,
You can have courage and not be afraid!
The story about Joshua is there so you'll know
The Lord God is with you WHEREVER YOU GO![9]

<hr />

[8] Deuteronomy 4:31 (ESV), "For the LORD your God is a merciful God. He will not leave you or destroy you or forget the covenant with your fathers that he swore to them."

[9] Joshua 1:9 (NLT), "This is my command—be strong and courageous! Do not be afraid or discouraged. For the LORD your God is with you wherever you go."

PRAYER OF SALVATION

If you would like to accept Jesus as your savior, pray a prayer like the one below. Then tell a trusted pastor or Christian friend so they can help you on your journey to knowing and following Jesus!

Dear God,

I know that you created me and want me to obey you with all my heart. I know I have disobeyed you. I have thought and done things against your directions. I am sorry. I know that you gave up your son Jesus, a perfect sacrifice, to save me from these sins and make me your child again. I accept your promises and ask you to please save me now and forever. Amen.

ABOUT THE AUTHOR

Alexis Davis has a love of learning, an undeniable rapport with children (of all ages), and a passion for the Word of God that is evident in all areas of her life. As the mother of a bright, perceptive boy, a volunteer for the children's ministry in her church home, and a veteran high school English teacher, she shares the love of Jesus with all those entrusted to her care. A native of Summerville, South Carolina, she treasures bringing *well-loved* things back to life—be it old furniture with a fresh coat of paint or a well-known Bible verse with a fresh, rhythmic story. She hopes and prays that through her stories, children and families will come to learn, love, and hide the Word of God in their hearts.

CPSIA information can be obtained
at www.ICGtesting.com
Printed in the USA
BVHW021449120821
614281BV00019B/985